A RARE BUT POSSIBLE CONDITION

A RARE BUT POSSIBLE CONDITION

ALISON DAVIS

SADDLE ROAD PRESS

Saddle Road Press
Ithaca, New York
saddleroadpress.com

Book design by Don Mitchell
Cover image by Alison Davis
Author photo by Tony Davis

ISBN 9798990054363
Library of Congress Control Number: 2024952893

v1.01

For Richard Rohr, who helps me grow a new heart every time the one I have gets broken.

Contents

I

II

III

I

DRAFT: HOW TO OVERCOME WRITER'S BLOCK (V.16)

have you tried writing with your feet?
the alphabet is
different that way, it's jagged and pregnant
or unrecognizable and commanding
such that what you already know is obscured
so that the S can
speak
slither
and show you the shorthand for infinity
turned up on its side
don't read a book that's for sure other's words will
seem so pretty and polished and you will forget how
the tides had their way with them for years,
thus wrongly wishing you would be washed out right now to
where the meaning is
because you will resurface and cough up nothing but foam
the wreck can't be reached this way

take out a map—only if it's accordion-style
cumbersome and you could never fold it back up the way it was
that's the kind of paths we chart with words,
all unfolding and changing creases and
rearranging what is face to face and back to back until
the front turns up again up but the insides got lost on the way
to an unmapped
destination
imagine the places instead, what kind of fountain
stands in that town square
and how many children are tossing their pennies in it
while their mothers scold *hurry up*
and if the first rain drop falls on the lip or on the
turbid surface

write it anyway even if it means nothing
especially if it means nothing

and of course don't erase
like you're talking on the phone to a friend
but back in the day when fingers and cords
were made for each other for twirling and embracing
write it just like that the paper is your friend
on the other end of the line and the words can't be deleted
and even if you feel like saying i'm sorry
the connection isn't so strong in a small irresolute voice
just keep the conversation going

because poems are for you
they feed you you deserve to be
at the head of the table
and taking seconds first this time
and the mashed words and sauteed verbs
fill the utilitarian room with the redolence of spices and
truth
truth doesn't have to be gourmet focus instead
on all the fixings
but if you still feel like you need a recipe
maybe consult
Roget or Merriam one more time

don't try to make it clean

starting and finishing are closer than they seem

Some More Urgent Than Others

Are there any common birth defects in soldier beetles?
Which of my neighbors is practicing the flute at sunrise?
How hot is too hot? What were you dreaming
about during the Great Conjunction of 2020, and
did it come true for you like it did for me? Can what these

people say and what those people say ever be reconciled?
Is there a more elegant way to slow down a reader than by
using italics? How many times must I be beheaded?
Why are we still so keen on the Pythagorean Theorem but
dismiss his views on the immortality of souls? If this poem

contained a set of compassion imperatives (such as:
mail someone a handwritten thank you card; scatter
wildflower seeds in a median; stand at the door to
hold it open for twenty-three people; forgive yourself
for that mistake you made when you were too young

to know better; kiss a tree, a flower, a hand), would you do
them? Why am I still picking up every feather that I see,
even the spindly ones caked with dirt? Did the nurse cry
when she got home? Who else can feel the Crown of
Thorns in the prickle of sweat when climbing a steep hill?

Which of the Greek words for love is most appropriate
here? Is it time to tell the truth yet? How many Kaw River
tributaries have I dipped my toes in, and how long
before the next flood? Does he keep in touch with anyone
from his cell block? What if we changed the name

from tinnitus to detecting the music of the spheres?
Could this vibration be what Galway Kinnell
meant about hearing *your whole existence?*

Berry Picking

My daughters rush toward
the thicket, arms outstretched.
their cries of joy start
in their hearts move up through
their eyes pour out of their mouths.
They snap the blackberries
from their prickly stems, push back
the thorny tangles in search of more
Sweetness. The juice stains
their fingers, lips, drips down their
chins. The palette of their childhood,
The wild canvas of skin.
Will they remember how beautiful
they were, made up in summer's colors,
how good their bodies were
on the side of the busy road, lost in
fruits? The sky their only
mirror, their reflections vast and
untamed. When one day their friends,
surely just a few short revolutions from now,
want to meet at the drugstore to
hold up lipsticks and rouge against
their faces, will they know the perfection they came from?
Will the scratch of brambles on their bodies
still call to them like a treasure map
they want to follow? Will the summer sap
still run strong? For now, they sing
   give thanks to the Mother Gaia
and laugh in the face of mystery.

FAR FROM HOME

My mother drove fourteen hours
to cut her father's fingernails and tell
stories about the last time they danced
the polka and ate dill pickle soup.
The framed photographs
on the wall will keep their shape
much longer than our bodies.
For months, my father turned his mother over
in the twin bed, just off the kitchen,
and readied himself to change the sheets.
Water was pouring from her legs, a rare
but possible condition, like living. They never
put her in a home. They were brave
enough to befriend the end. And here we are
again among the Mysteries. Tremendous

and trembling. It has been over a year
since I heard my brother's voice,
since he stood in the doorway with a knife
in his hands, since he sent the picture
with a gun to his head,
daring a devil only he could see.
We prayed so much in those days,
those days when the last green promises
of spring rotted on the vine. We pray
now too, in the Eagles Lodge where the
meetings are held, in the churches it's easy
to make fun of. Tragedy rouses us
in a way that beauty is jealous
of. Have we ever known what to do
with these things that never

grew? The children learn our habits.
They gasp at the fawn in the meadow and
tiptoe over, whispering

"she's looking at me!"
They ask to skip rocks in the creek
where the steelhead trout lay
their eggs. Sometimes at night, they rage
in their sleep. We hold
and behold the churning of the generations
in the blink between fifteen and fifty.
One auntie leaves her husband, the other
doesn't. The new dog is named after the old one.
When there are too many empty bottles
at the gathering, I go out walking alone in the rain.
It stays green here all year. There are always geraniums
in bloom. The puddles turn sky into drinkable light.

BLOODLINES

Vicki was the first to get her period, but we didn't know. What is it like to be given the lead, especially one you weren't particularly interested in taking? We spread rumors about why she wouldn't get in the hot tub at the hotel in Montreal. Our faces were steamed pink. We repeated jokes about sex that none of us understood. When she confronted us with a surprisingly mature biological explanation, we laughed uncomfortably. Who else dreamed about blood rivers that night?

✕

I heard that you weren't supposed to work out when you got your period. Or maybe I'd heard that people could tell you were wearing a pad when you had gym shorts on, that it would give you diaper butt, and they would be grossed out. But that cute boy was supposed to be staffing the front desk that day. He used Sun In to bleach his hair and wore cargo shorts with pockets so big I could fit most of my dreams in them. Rachel helped me cover the tampon applicator in Vaseline, coached me on how to insert it. No one will know now. Sit-ups. Crunches. Push-ups. Light jog. It didn't feel right. I went home, pulled the plug, cried into my floral bedsheets.

✕

It is known that Savannah free bleeds. Really, though, it is known that she is free. She sings like a mountain casting off a thick mist and wears whatever she wants. Her freckles are constellations so bold that if you look carefully enough, you can read your whole future on her face. I first met her when she was fifteen. We were reading a Shuntaro Tanikawa poem, and she decided it was fine to stand out from the crowd, even if it made other people uncomfortable.

✕

Iman spent a week sewing reusable cotton and flannel pads to send to a non-profit in sub-Saharan Africa. Can you imagine not being able to go to school because your moon-body needed to take a walk down to earth? I wonder what rituals around this crimson honey have been lost, left behind, dislocated, unlanded. Iman's father came here with soul-screams and bone-sighs and different memories of bloodshed. Their minds clash. At Eid a few years back, she said she couldn't pray because she was on her period. *Is that what you really believe?* She covered her head and started to recite.

✕

At the lip of the creek, I kneel down and spill my cup onto the ground. I swish my bandana in the water and scrub it against the gravel. An old teacher once told me that blood is the most spiritual form of matter. I think of Jesus on the cross. I think of the bobcat born just days ago. Does everything on the inside eventually make its way out? Is the earth big enough to receive it all?

✕

Joan paced around the office, waiting for her period to come. *Please don't be pregnant, please don't be pregnant.* Relief at the blood in the toilet. Megan paced up and down the hallway of her starter home, praying her period wouldn't come. *Please be pregnant, please be pregnant.* Devastation at the blood in her pajamas. As soon as I night-weaned my child, my period returned. My mother got a hysterectomy and couldn't walk for a month. Her unused pads heaped on top of the junk mail in the trash. We are all wading through brackish waters. Our bodies are the roots we trip on. Our bodies are the bridges we use to get across.

✕

Eli cries when he gets his period and refuses to come to school. Once, he locked himself in the car and wouldn't come out until the blood was gone. The endurance of a body swells in proportion to the spirit. What about when the spirit cannot fit in the body? Camellia blossoms fell all around him, and he dreamed himself into a sketchbook where he could be pink and soft and would no longer need to question the seasons. His parents think the pill caused him to have seizures. We are all learning what is true.

20

X

The paper is thin and flecked with pulp. Nammy's chapbook slumbers on my desk. She wrote about ghosts and tenderness. She wrote an ode to menstruation. In this world where easy is a marketing ploy and affections come and go with the traffic, she lavishes love on her body, the hard way. Which is to say the real way. Which is also to say, she thinks she's doing it wrong. We're perhaps too familiar with our own blood, the two of us, and we still write to each other in red ink.

X

The door has been locked, and Naomi goes home. She had to turn many women away. No more diapers, no more feminine products. First it was the formula, and now this. She cries at the immensity of the need in the world, at the crookedness of our systems. She connects to her own infinity. *You are vast*, she tells herself. Still, on the bathroom scale, she weighs herself again, trying not to be obsessive. She takes off all her clothes, relieved that the number dips a little. A small drop of blood trickles down her thigh and lands on the 7's shoulder. Is this a story about losses and gains?

How to Greet a Hypocrite

tell stories about weddings
& fig trees
write nothing down
except with a stick
in the sand

wait for the hosannas to die
down; such earth-bound enthusiasm
will soon exhaust itself
in silence & silence
is necessary

feel the river in your body,
the one you were born in
& splash in what you can never
hold in your hand

what was true at the beginning?
light & darkness & labor &
destruction & striving:
say that

condense the fear into a ball,
a marble you can hold
under your tongue
swallow everything else whole,
but let the body dissolve
that fear

put on your bridegroom's
garments & dance
your movement on the roof
of the world in the sun
of your skin is a perpetually
relevant message

LOVE LITANY

The balcony. The backyard. The bend in the road.
The hole in the bush where the baby fox
disappeared and where we started
to hear the birds again last spring. This is a litany.
This is a litany of all the places where love has touched me.
The bus from north campus on which I watched
Susannah every morning, how full her lips still
look in my memory. Pont Neuf, alone, at eighteen.
At the electric mango sunrise of wherever here happens
to be. While over-mixing the batter of a
poorly proportioned cake. In a church meeting room
where everyone there wants to believe it's possible
to love an alcoholic, or at least love in a less painful
way. Big Basin, before during after the waterfall's
slick rocks. Out at the American Legion with a father
who doesn't know how to grow old but is anyway.
Asilomar sunset under a shared blanket.
Every step between his seat and mine, in an overly
air-conditioned classroom in an overly
oppressive land on the brink of the jasmine
revolution. On stage, thanking you all for coming.
In my bed, making a baby. In my bed,
birthing a baby. Big Sur at dawn with nothing to my name.
In an amphitheater full of Orthodox-enough Jews being
lectured on the dangers of intermarriage. This is
still a litany. This is still a litany about being touched
by love, which has so many strange
hands and no sense of decorum whatsoever
and who will reach out in the middle of crowded airport
terminal and show up on the face of a nun in her
ill-fitting scapular and olive wood rosary while strangers
gawk and stare but I know what wild faith clothes
her, holds her.

It's Not a Race

We run past the bungalow with the blue shutters
where I grew up and learned

that safety is relative and love has more hands
than the ones that wrap the towel

around a shivering body and fry the bologna
and reach for the paddle because

no one ever taught them otherwise. We run
past the field where proud Black bodies

perform calisthenics, and I think of Grace
and her red barrettes in Mr. Halowicki's gym

We run past dueling flags that proclaim which
lives matter and boarded up liquor shops and

the motel my dad said the prostitutes lived in
but I don't know if I believe that and now there

is an allotment garden out back with towering
sunflowers and bean tendrils spiraling themselves

up to the sky. We run into women mowing lawns
who say hello and women chatting on porches

who say hello and a man washing his car who
does not but we greet him anyway. We don't know

anyone here now, but we know the houses and
too many of the stories they hold in their bones.

The real estate trends say white flight, and yes,
where I am, flying through the streets where

I don't belong but maybe could trying to understand
with each pavement strike what it means

to be from a place where there was still a dirt
road behind the Methodist church where racial

slurs were common parlance and where I was
taught I was white. I run deeper into a history

I haven't learned how to hold, into envy for those
who can own a home, who rebuilt this

neighborhood when abandoning it was the obvious
option, when the meager but not insignificant

privilege packed its bags and went looking for
larger lawns and a two-car garage.

We don't run past the Lebanese bakery where
Salem Haddad's family bought their bread or

the factory where my father worked nights
with his bare hands in industrial ink

we never thought twice about until he got cancer.
We circle back again to the blue shutters, to grandma's

house next door. She's dead, grandpa's dead, but
the house has a fresh coat of paint and geraniums

in the planter box. I roller skated in that driveway
and weeded the rose garden. The house was always

clean and tidy. We wipe our sweat. It starts to rain,
and the sky stutters and sobs all over our bodies.

Every breath is heavy with memory, heavy with
whatever it is we can still feel but will never

understand. We run until my dad says he's done
but then decide to take one more lap around

the neighborhood to see what else we've forgotten
to remember.

Missing Monarchy

1.
There is a natural intimacy
between earth and sky
that the wing-beings are trying
to whisper to us. Where
is the quiet that will let me hear?

2.
Beside the small soda spring
where the bubbling water tastes of blood,
we streak our faces with red-
orange clay. A student hands me
a wing of a monarch butterfly.
I feel like this is something
you'd want to touch, she says,
and she is right. Like a feather,
soft, miraculous.

3.
We plant milkweed and cosmos.
Then marigold and aster. We wait.
This is a kind of prayer.

4.
The buddleias of memory
have all dried up in the summer
haze. Sun unrelenting. We were almost
on a quest for purple. What's left
of their small petals turns
to dust between my fingers.
The butterflies that once feasted
here have not moved on,
they are simply gone. Loving
in this world entails significant
grief.

5.
I stand in front of a mural
in Pacific Grove. Black and orange fan
out like my two hands, which open,
asking, in all this confusion, what
can remain? Hubris wants us
to be saviors. Humility wants us
to be a part of Every Thing
that is saving itself.

Revolutions in Meaning

1a. an orbital motion about a point, esp. as distinguished from an axial rotation

The dictionary cannot make visible to me the difference between orbital and axial. I wonder if she could. I wonder if she could hold something in her hands, cast it in the role of a lifetime as The Great Turning, and take no credit for having directed this cosmic spectacle. She is not here now though. I scour the diagrams, static images on a screen of what is meant to be in motion, what cannot possibly stand still, ask my eyes to extend the movement of the arrows from their two-dimensional depiction and into my three-dimensional life. I cross-reference astronomical explanations and charts and equations with variables I have never encountered. What else have I never encountered? I vaguely grasp that one can be moving forward while still being pulled back— or is it elsewhere or is it away? Timidly I allow my body to feel its own orbital path. Can I call it a revolution?

1b. A turning or rotational motion about an axis

I picture a carnival ride, the teacups. The grimy wheel in the center. The built-in bench that goes all the way around the inside, perfect for sliding. Gather your friends, hand over your tickets, it's time to twirl. Mechanical belching. Achy and overused joints of machinery screech to life, give a little jolt. The cups, outstretched on tentacular metal arms, start to rotate like the second hand on a clock, jumpy for just a moment, then smooth. Some kind of column in the middle that tethers us all together, the center around which we spin. It would have been enough to just circle like this, but carnivals are not for subtlety or leaving well enough alone. Hands hit the wheel and crank, unlicensed and reckless drivers on a non-existent road. A second kind of rotation splishes and splashes the bodies inside the mirthful teacup. Clockwise, counterclockwise. One revolution after another, until someone yells stop. I was always the one who yelled stop. I was always the one who couldn't stand steady on solid ground after the dismount.

1c. A single complete cycle of such orbital or axial motion

I formed each from the inside, stood enclosed by my creation. One rock at a time, the fire pit emerged from my effort. One rock at a time, the medicine wheel birthed itself through my body. One rock at a time, the altar woven with sky and sand through my hands. One rock at a time, the zero held its ground and signaled the end of the countdown. There is no more waiting. The revolution is here.

2. The overthrow and replacement of a government

Which versions are real? The unfolding of events that can't be tucked back into the envelope. The revolutionary breath that can't be put back into King's lungs. Gandhi bowing at the crowd as he went down. Spirits that can't be incarcerated belonging to bodies that can. Laulupidu because words are weapons and songs are slick cannonballs slicing through the air. Dessalines carrying out the last days of the scorched earth campaign. Freedom fires lick the world back into its wild. The Republic's renaming of the months while there was still blood on the cobblestones of the public square. There is still blood in the public square. Who showed up and why? Who is interviewing the human heart, recording its rhythms and skipped beats, playing back its testimony on the evening news, as evidence that there are still revolutions we can't not believe in?

3. A sudden or momentous change in situation

Yesterday I had hair; today I have stubble. This morning, I hung the damp clothes out on the balcony, and this afternoon they are dry; at what moment did they cross over? As a teenager, I snuck out of the hotel room on 42nd Street and wrote about never wanting to marry or have children or need other human beings; these days I reside in the whorl of these universes of relationality. Under an absurdly blue sky on Montara Mountain, I promised myself to never miss another panorama; how many days, like today, have I chosen to stay under the covers? Once, for the longest once, I feared my own body, other bodies, all bodies, any body, everybody; then I didn't. In fact, right this very moment, I summon my desire and my dry bones rise up to fight for what they were fearfully and wonderfully made to feel. Are any of these revolutions? I don't know what it means to see something as sudden or momentous when my eyes are forged out of such aeons.

4. *Geology* A time of major crustal deformation, when folds and faults are formed

Would you read articles written in the 1830s about the moral and religious truths contained in the earth's strata? Samuel Metcalf was trying to find his way past the commercial extraction of valuable resources. Geology traced a new fault line between the mineral and the almighty. All along, every atom, whether from the flax and the chaff or the volcanic crust, has been speaking out of deep time. Anyone who hears recapitulates the revolution, is shaped into something new.

THIRST

I rushed through
the Châtelet station
with all the others,
sped across the moving walkway
in sync with the crowd.
I saw a mother struggle
with her bulky stroller,
and a gray-bearded man
in a djellaba clinging
to the handrail
as commuters shoved
through. I didn't slow down.

I snaked my way
toward the table
with all the others.
We always assumed there
would be enough, if not
more. I loaded my plate
like everyone else. Roasted
potatoes and fresh berries.
I went for seconds. Grilled
asparagus, key lime pie.
I ate more than my fill. I wrote
a thank you note to the waiter
on the back of the receipt, but
the bus boy cleared it, along
with enough leftovers
from my fellow diners to
feed many hungry men.

I stood in line
on the lip of the curb
with all the others.
When it started to rain,

I opened my umbrella
and asked my neighbor
if she wanted to duck
under with me. She smiled,
said yes. We didn't speak
beyond that moment.
I watched a few others rehearse
this delicate ritual.
I watched many more
undefended against the downpour.

Aren't we all
always of at least two hearts?
In the end, like the others, I have
sometimes thirsted for goodness,
and sometimes I have pursed my lips
and turned away.

A Bike Commuter's Modest Use of Democracy

Dear civil servant, this message is addressed to you
Because
The mornings are so precarious: finger clouds are
Scratching the sky and hoarfrost cloaks wrap the
Black earth
Yes, yes, of course this is not your purview
But context can be a heartening thing for
Those of us who do not take to the roads armored
Commandeering large vessels
Relying on satellite navigational systems
In an attempt to outsmart
The trail of marching
Red ants inching toward the next intersection,
So as you read on
Remember
We take it on our cheeks, me and my kin
We take it in our lungs, it burns sometimes
Both the rime and the coughing barges
But boldly do we go in our thirteen inches of
Not-quite-ditch
Using sleepy muscles and keen seeing and hoping
Our phosphorescent vests are enough to
Keep from not existing at the strike of some ungodly
Continental tread
You see, the city has a workforce I'm told, brooms
And callused hands and care for
Common welfare and pride in what We can do
So what can we do
About this narrow runway from which our spokes
And such never take off
Rather just keep landing one revolution after another
Over backwashed and persistent debris
(the wind has been throwing tantrums
in her old age, not unlike those
small, sweet-cheeked creatures that have been

strapped in styrofoam-lined seats
of my racing passersby)
Between you and me, I have only just learned
To balance
I have only just found my pace
What I am asking for is help
Staying safe

Moving On

I wrap the framed photograph of the Garden
of Gethsemane in a fleece blanket, secure it
with remnants of yarn. I do the same with
the Van Gogh poster, the canvas print of my daughter

and niece running into a summer sunset. I layer
the few ceramic plates with washcloths and wrap
the mugs in dish towels. We save money this way,
and spare the trash bin too. A man I admire says

to leave it all and buy what we need when we get
there. He says the cost of labor alone is more than
what it would take to stock the kitchen secondhand,
find a desk, a couch. But his calculations fail to

account for the fact that the labor is mine, the hours
mine, the heave and heft mine, and the pay nothing
more than a chance to touch a few raw memories
one last time before saying goodbye. Parallel lines

of light stripe the bedroom floor. My younger daughter
was born here, beside the balcony, from my belly to
my arms to my bed in one miraculous breath.
Every evening, no matter the weather, the hills

were coated in honey-shine. The laundry hung out
to dry, while days became years. A kitchen full of
neighborhood children, batches of blueberry muffins
with lemon zest, cheaper than store-bought, and

we all passed the bowl around to lick clean what's left
of the batter. Simple pleasures for pennies. Flatbreads
frying in smoking oil. Green onion cuttings growing back
in a jar on the shelf. The landlord comes to negotiate

our exit, part of a greater exodus. *You're right to get out.*
It's time you bought a place of your own, as his wife
takes our money and deducts for the stains in the carpet.
I teach to fill my heart, not my pocketbook, I joke,

and we've been on a single income since the pandemic.
My dad dreams of going halves on a house on a lake
where we spend our summers, where we gather
for Christmas, where we keep the radio tuned to a station

that plays Cat Stevens. It would be nice, I think, as I put down
the security deposit and first month's rent, a full month's salary,
on our new rental. There's a small cluster of redwood trees in the
sliver of space off the bedroom.

The American River's just a walk away. I don't
know what it means to be borrowing my way through
this world full of grief and exuberance. I turn my ears to
what the trees say about home.

Distant Galaxies

When given a chance to look through the lens
into the unknown, I find an eccentric cast
of beloved characters: Birth canals, the ultimate un-tombs,
always dilating, always leading to the light.
The inside of a buttonhole. Dreamed mountainscapes
in which we keep saying yes and mean it every time.
The glazed over left eye of the blind man
in front of the mosque on Avenue Bourguiba.
A trail of Jelly Bellys, caramel corn and
crushed pineapple, dropped in the night
Arcade carpet. Sparklers against the sky on Diwali,
spelling out each of our names.
What's under the four-poster bed.
Golden-rimmed singing bowls, forever ringing,
resonating. Handless fingerprints of faith,
signature of heaven.
The cliff from which Kierkegaard leapt
when he decided to be born.
Glittered bodies on the dance floor, pulsing.
Fireflies over Abilene. Bioluminescence
in the slough, deeper and deeper down.
The floaters behind my closed eyes at midnight,
at 2, and 2:18, and so on. Flecks of summer solstice
from the raspberry patch. Cosmic grains of sand.
Marbled ceiling, vaulted out of the Great Collision.
Mirror of insatiable desire.
The fixed itinerary it's time to abandon.
More proof that there is no such thing as no-thing.
Another new iteration of Rumi's field.
My mind keeps adjusting. I keep seeing more of
what we used to call invisible.

CELEBRATIONS
for and with Nammy

This is a day to celebrate scotch
tape dispensers, those exoskeletal spool
stores with tiny jagged plastic teeth
that have of late replaced the ferocious
metal fangs of old
indiscriminately doling out almost opaque
ribbon (that takes upon itself my fingerprint
before) it binds the page of *Atlas of a Difficult World*
that would otherwise have been lost and
affixes on the stucco walls a single sepia
memory
of the summer
before the Arab Spring

Today let us bless the late train
the slumbering steel giant not yet lumbering
into the overwhelmed station
with my soured brow I can't be coaxed to
wait without consulting the obtuse timetable
unlaminated underappreciated
and scan the platform for signs of mechanical life
instead a run appears in the stockings on an
exquisite leg follow those unassuming tracks
instead spend time on that trajectory instead it is going
somewhere without a clock

Today let us exalt the briefest of
communions, olive tree branching into sky
your hand slipping into mine
flickering aeroplane lights within
distant earthbound eyes
slender breastbone muffling
her thirsty infant's cries
and the moonlit rivulets returning desperately

between archipelagos of footprinted sand
to salty high tides under pregnant nights

Today let us venerate long distance
phone-calls, lines
that almost convey the glow of your voice
the carved wooden box full of careworn letters
written decades ago, slightly yellowed within
her bedside table
crowds of patient halves waiting
in airport gates, cardboard signs saying
"thank god, you're home"

Today let me thank the creaking steps
leading to your open front door,
where nostalgia and maddening traffic
end with your eyes boring into mine
and here at last are you, old friend
weathered by life perhaps,
but radiating warmth that
has only grown
with time

II

WORDS OFFERED

like a fish released from a makeshift hook, flapping
    around on the deck of a dinghy.
        as crooked as a curse jutting out from

between clenched teeth.
    caving in around the edges, like an orange
        that needs to be eaten right away

before it rots, before it descends into the ground
    from which it sprang.
        whipping a rippled surface into a slow,

thick foam, as a cargo ship cutting across the ocean.
    like lion's breath, up close
        like a bouquet of tulips bought of a whim and

offered to a friend, a stranger, a gravestone, a window sill.
    How do we choose to break
                        the silence?

Summer Winds Nursery

pot me in something slick / & blue
something wide / & round & warm
like your mouth

rub me between your / palms
like a sprig of rosemary / stalk of lavender

teach me my other names / scientific
tongue twisters / pseudonyms
mispronounce me but say me

touch me slowly / softly & lightly
like lamb's ear
when the ragged edges of / morning close in on you

protect my roots from / frost-
filled exchanges of stubborn fears &

grow with me

THROWING SEEDS AT ROCKS

i take the seeds in my hand. they tickle, settle into the lines in my palm, stick to my skin. they are heavy and light, heavy and light, heavy and light. i start to practice a gentle, steady breath. receive and release. soon, i will blow all these seeds loose. soon. i will send them on their way, knowing their way is not *away*. you are not going *away*.

i have read the instructions on each packet. mound spacing, seed depth, indoor sowing for when the outside world seems too harsh to support new life. i took note of sensitivities to root disturbances and soil drainage indications. i read botanical names aloud, each an incantation, each a celebration of the mystery of growth, how we dare to name it, even before we know what it means, if we ever can truly know what it means. i tracked the adjectives — pungent, smooth, dazzling, stiff, mature — and the promises of the harvests to come. none of this is the matter at hand, the matter in my hand.

today i have come to do what i don't know by opening my fist and letting go.

i will share every *red* seed I have ever loved in us, with unshakeable faith in where it came from and its Grand Return. *scarlet emperor* words, spoken into enormous silences and vaulted hopes. *red burgundy okra* heartaches that turned into trading paintings long into the night. *drop dead red sunflower* summer afternoons when everything was in bloom. *scarlet gleam nasturtium* and *scarlet o'hara morning glory* footsteps over the wood chips, around the mulberry tree, beside the black cumin. *celosia chief red flame* glances traded when we thought no one else was looking. *empress of india nasturtium* eulogies of the ones we couldn't keep alive, *red amposta* heartbeats, layers of pulsing and throbbing and thrumming and singing and and and and. *red kuri winter squash* promises of surviving the cold, of the warmth within. *oriental brilliant red poppy* sketches of forms i am just beginning to perceive with you.

i have given myself over to you in so many red ways,
red, the color of my own deep blood that i am learning
to keep.

but we're bigger than just these shades. we are also *broken colors four o'clock* drawings in the sand and dust. remember how i danced myself into the surf while you watched? it took you until asilomar to know what garrapata had already shown me. the lilies guarded my secret. we are also *milkweed hello yellow* songs and strumming patterns, feel how those *songbird delight* chords teach us to touch and intersect. watch these seeds waltz right out of my palm.

watch me release the moments that are bigger than color itself. i can release them because i know they could never leave me. *bright lights swiss chard* airport runs in your first year away. *halo hollyhock* paper bag treasures. *glorious gleam nasturtium* walks around the block, with or without an agenda. *bright lights cosmos* game night at the donut shop, one scrabble tile at a time. *torch tithonia* magazine envelopes, postage paid, solar eclipse stamps, the thrill of seeing my name in your handwriting. all of these *bring home the butterflies* moments are initiations. look how many new loves we are starting when we give away the *impatiens midnight blend* of skin on skin.

i feel the vastness of our beginnings. i will not yield to the temptation to try and control them. i am willing to scatter *coreopsis double sunburst* embraces when the sky blushes and the light breaks through, as if just for us. *blazing star* harmonies that were years in the making. *sensation double click blend* and *sensation cosmos* sharing clothes and writing poems and driving narrow roads. *phlox grandiflora starry eyes blend* blessed reticences, because here we are now with such courage, here in such precious obliteration, entwined among the riddles of the astronomer's world. how can i not read the rest inside you when you are splattered across the sky and keep revealing new constellations every time i look up?

You teach me the *keepsake* of the *lace flower*,
promise me the *perennial* of the *bloom*,
put the *wild* of the *arugula* on my tongue.

Tanka Series Before Sunrise

she listens, ponders
she speaks in red marigolds
and garlands of clouds
precious presence redeeming
what time labored to reveal

      X

undress me each day
clothe me with your wild mercy
shear my hair as well
what am I still afraid of?
my old life is heaped on the floor

      X

the story is new
the experience is not
my god, what is this
galloping feeling in my
formerly terrified heart?

December

1.
I can lose everything.
Can I lose everything?
Will I lose everything?

2.
I shaved my head like a monk, life a mourner
in a public display of grief

3.
I dreamed I was sucking on stones, explaining how odd it is
that you need a hammer to make a hammer.
The glass was not half-full, not half-empty;
it was refillable, and I kissed her.

4.
The desert's persistent thirst is not
desperationing.
The jungle's misty breath not
proudifying.
                          Can I learn to love (myself)   like that?

5.
Plant stars in a
furrowed brow of earth,
crystallized in
winter frost.
There is enough light.

In the Liminal Mo(u)rning

Can you hear me? None of us asked to be recruited into this
nighttime rigamarole. No mantras or breaths counted or tracing
of the moon's perichoresis can save me from

waking into the morning I dread. This is the season where the
birch in the neighbor's yard is vermillion by seven and amber
just moments later, and I'm the only one I can share

it with. So I might as well celebrate it, solitude slathered all over
my still-here soul. Love and loss have proved their relativity on
this earth. Still, I try to sing on key, lyrics of

something unconditional I once tasted: *forever* for this body is an
attempt blessed to fail; definitive doesn't exist in these cells. I
stumble to the kitchen to take the tinctures and bow

down. Those with some roots of tenderness beneath all the strain
will seek me out. I burn in a fresh fire and strum myself open.
Beware of the light streaming out of my hands.

Rehearse the Ritual

Today I have no discernable age,
am a word without an etymology,
an expression without

                            an origin.

Between what she promised with her body
and what I now grieve in mine
is a language carved back into silence,
a relief disappearing back into the frieze.

Did we ever match?
Were we ever telling the same story?

I light the candle. I rehearse
the ritual. *Spirit, bless and*

                            release.

Only my hands on my heart.
Only my breath in my ear.

FEBRUARY 8, 2022

She wrote *my lover has breasts*
soft as gunpowder.
I wrote *we speak the language*
of coming back from the brink.
We wrote our way to Rumi's field.

      ✳

I can teach you how to sing
while beheaded.
The blood is a sheet
music of sorts.
My mouth is perfect
ly intact. Are you
listening?

      ✳

In my dreams, I can dance-fly.
I watched them make the instruments
out of sheets of metal, hammers, and nails.
We walked up the stairs and into
a basement. There were mattresses
on the floor, and we crowded around.
He danced. She sang. I saw their former
faces, the way they used to shine
when people believed in them. I felt the dance
that brought me to them. The closeness,
the touching, the movement, the breath.
I was not ashamed. I was meant to bring
them back into the light the light.
When their performance was over, I took
his head into my hands. I told him I could

still see what he was, which is what he is.
I told him I would help the others.

      X

The liver produces bile to carry
away waste. I am wasting away.
I can't bring myself to trace
the form on the page.

      X

I practice being my future
self by mentally composing
notes to the alive and
unalive beings I meet
on my walk around the neighborhood.
Dear wavy cactus,
Dear abandoned blue flannel shirt,
Dear empty paint can,
I am here with you.

      X

Two diagrams.
One radial, bursting out, exploding.
One a soft cradle, space carved out of a periphery.
One the tire, the other the spokes.
Do they not together form a wheel?
I turn this all over in my mind.

LOST ARTIST

I am an artist. My medium is loss.
I didn't choose this path to pay the bills
but rather to be a willing chambermaid
to what is. Why should I fear this
wide and wild truth: loss is just the face
of impermanence that we must learn
to love if we are to call ourselves
of this world.

I practice my art every day. I make masterpieces
of misplaced papers with half-written poems
about pruning shears and crucifixions
and untongued tales of the woman at the well
alone at high noon, which is to say me,
bereft of all respectable relation
and just shy of dying
of thirst.

I ready my installation for my upcoming exhibit,
Voices from the Void, which consists of a silent
recitation of the destinations I never found
on the map whose boundaries were erased
on the day I let my body become the bridegroom
of doom.

Because of who I love
I lost my security my sanity my safety
my stability, my ability to laugh more often
than cry, then I cry about losing the business card
with the blockprint that I would have handed out to
aspirers and admirers who want to revere
these works of mine before they too
lose the thread and unravel,
naked in the street.

I artfully lost my claim to the rivers and the roads
between a past I was on the path to redeeming
and a framable future that felt one brushstroke
away from finished. I lost a brother
who lost his sobriety who lost a father who
lost his faith, lost a family who lost their names
when I disavowed mine. I draw the disappearance
of desire, sign FIAT in the corner, and give it
away for free.

My pièce de résistance is spinning
the loss of my beloved
whose precious body matched mine
into such a beloved loss
on a silver wheel with spokes made of feathers,
my unlocatable heart my signature centerpiece
around which this revolution turns
until in the center there is peace,
born from what walks and talks like disaster
but whose belly is as soft as sycamore
leaves.

MORE THAN

for Joan Didion

grief-weaver, i came to you years ago
with a dreamdark question, one that is
still soaring through these winter nights
so far from their own blue,
a question that declines at every turn
to comply with the story
i thought i was going to be writing.
a question like the santa ana,
building pressure off the coast,
ready to incinerate what we are
trying to call home: a stretch of beach,
an open-air kitchen, a body.

If I had seen that it could end, what would I have done differently?

grief-teller, i listened to what you said
about life changing in an instant, which you
turned into an accursed incantation
with those haunting italics. what was
there left to do but live like them, askew,
walking at a slant, the way they did
across the page? i am willing to limp.
the drafts piled up on the edge of my desk,
and i sat at the table of my hollow bones
alone. your deconstructed, reconstructed,
unconstructable chronologies are
excruciatingly accessible, which means
i must light the tapers, put on my apron,
and prepare a meal for one.

The craziness is receding but no clarity is taking its place.

grief-bearer, you scoffed at the aspirin
advertisements and their omnipresent promise

that we can outsmart death. my grandmother
swears by head cheese on marble rye
and hangs rosary beads on her doorknob. her
life has been as complicated as the canals
in central valley, a willed geography of tempting nature,
so as not to say forcing fate, full of thick-knuckled
certainty in everything that could be built, even as
she buried her teenage son. i also placed my
youth in an early grave. like you, can i
write my way out of this oblivion? who else
believes in the place where the kissing never stops?

I look for resolution but find none.

grief has shaken all the colors
from the wheel. they no longer flow
into each other, and cadmium is overused.
even so, we have not grown colorblind.
so little is truly complementary in this life,
but we continue to fashion
our words just so.

WHAT SHE WANTS

she wants to see
    the softly stooping willow in bloom
    beside the river
she wants to hear
    god in the smallness of a stone
    in her daughter's hands
she wants to swallow
    fireflies and speak their light into the
    vast violent silence
she wants to stand
    on the bridge without wondering
    who else has already crossed it
she wants to believe
    that the vessel of her body is capable of something
    more precious than this
she wants to stretch
    from here to beyond where
    the breath stops
she wants to leave
    and stay gone until the earth exhales
    at first light and the sky goes
    lilac around the edges
she wants to disappear
    into the juniper bush and watch
    the seasons cycle
she wants to feel
    things she can't talk about, doesn't
    have the words to talk about
she wants the song of the conch
    the stillness of the grass
    the courage of the harp
    the weight of the future
    the promise of the shadow

she wants to let go
    of everything she's carrying
    but she doesn't know what else to do with
    her hands.

UNANNOUNCED GUEST

Oh, Hope, I wasn't expecting you. Now isn't really a good time. I'm quite busy at the moment. I have things to prepare. I am preparing things. Judging things. Pointing my finger at people because *this matters*, and I have to be the one to say it. Could you come back some other time, like when the peach tree I never planted starts to blossom? Or when the sidewalk turns into a tidepool? I should be done with my business by then. Well, since you insist, since there's something in your larksong voice that tastes like a meadow, I guess you can come in for a few minutes. Have a seat over there next to that stack of ledgers.

Hope, you are crowding me a little, and the way you smell like jasmine is distracting me. Was that you I saw one afternoon, outside the mosque, lying between the stray dog and the smiling blind man? His eyes were so milky-beautiful, but we can talk about that later. Right now, I'm trying to keep track of all these resentments. Someone stacked the cereal bowls out of order, and the meeting ran twenty minutes over. Also, didn't you hear the rumors? They threatened me. They called me dangerous, a predator. They found out I was thirsty and handed me a glass of bleach, hoping I would drink and be drained of all my color. They walked all over her. You saw the scars when you visited her, right? We need a list of every transgression. I absolutely must set the record straight. *These things matter*, Hope, don't they?

They don't? You don't know what you're talking about. You are so wrapped up in your beehive-thoughts. Not everything in the world is sweet, Hope. People take more than what they need. I guess you're right that some give, give, gratefulize even out of utter emptiness. I felt that way too, that morning by the field. But please, could you just let me finish what I'm working on? These records are my area of expertise. I could have a hit list put together in no time flat if you would just stop interfering. Why don't you make yourself some tea? By the time the water boils, I'll have the tallies ready: how many times I have been wronged, and how much each time hurt, so that I know how many times to twist the knife and how many eyes to pluck out. I have a good memory, Hope, and I'm good at writing. So I remember and write.

Yes, I do remember that night at the donut shop and painting coreopsis in the driveway, but I have more pressing accounts to detail, Hope. I don't have time to look back on my daughter's first birthday when my father was in good health and we walked the pier in Pacifica. The mountain in Montara doesn't matter now, nor does Sinai or Deauville. The way he carried me into the shower when I couldn't walk. The tablecloth patterned after the ceiling of the Blue Mosque. The full pot of navy bean soup. But the kissing that never stops stopped, Hope. Don't you see? I am determined to write down everything she could have said instead of that sincere *I'm sorry*. I'm trying to describe the devil that took over his eyes when he stood in the doorway with a knife in his hands. We used to play so well as kids. We used to help each other cheat in Monopoly. We walked to school arm-in-arm for years. It still rains in the summer there, in that place we are from. It stays green.

Don't go snooping around in those journals. Those other-lunged love letters to no one. Mere sour-lipped longings now. Transient truths. Vagabonds, vagrants. I know that I wrote about redemption. I know what I said about healing. Still, cancer claims, and the fires feast. I know Lucy never became an orphan and Luke built a new house, Kari too. I know I was in full bloom, but that season was short, and now I'm withering on the vine. You expect me to believe I'm the whole vineyard? Yes, I am surviving the frost. Hope, how can you see me shivering even now and still want to talk about the sun?

Okay, Hope, since you are so committed to covering me with garlands and filling the cracks with gold, let me level with you. My faith is sun-starved. I hobble on grease-fire feet. My hands are barley husks. It's cliffs all the way down. I jump and nothing catches me. I can't catch my breath. You want me to breathe with you? There's that jasmine again. The pink and white. The sidewalk that ran out, and the warmth that permanently stained my palms. The sea-song at the heart of all my psalms. I'm singing again, the waves are crashing, the boulders are eroding, the sun is setting fast. It's night it's dark I'm dark-deep in the belly of the unknown I groan I groan I grow-groan in the deep-dark in the dark the stars come out the stars and hope and Hope, they start to shout, they sing *hope.*

AND YET, THE WRECK

for Adrienne Rich

wordpurpose   wordmaps
change-one-letter-no-longer-word words
or too much word for what i too timidly mean
studiously chosen expand your vocabulary words
write your life, your
hardest sorrowwords
bury the one who was your husband words
yes the kaddish is tattered
but i taught my students how to do decoupage poems
and we made new life
from those burial coffin
words don't-know-how-to-be-whole-again
words we still don't know if Parker
is six feet under words or if he's cosmic flotsam
that's the wreck

the ladder is broken, the lexical
one i climb up and down with you
but you still put breath back into what can be said
so i fill my lungs with words you
taught me and just jump   dive
words bubble up down here below
and emerge in strange syllables
crenellate and flabellate
everything unfolding and trying to reveal
a pattern what do we need in order to be able
to see it? eyes eyes   yes but something
of your syntax too
short   short   punctuate   punch   pause
until you're unfamiliar with your own
life or familiar with it for the first time
either extreme serves the same end breaks
the bad habits we give words

sending love with heart   yes now
i see that i can and i must if there's to be
any vitality among us please

standing over the husband's grave
with a sturdy new breasted love
standing at the base of the berlin wall
after the war had been called
standing soul-cracked at the western wall
we're all
in mourning   who has the right words
to comfort us
memories maybe if we write them down
in the right order at the right time
or maybe just write what's left
to right what's left and
we're back in the wreck again

we're breathing while submerged again
we're sinking and then
watch the ocean dust settle in
places that light never touches
but our inner eye
touches them our words delineate
their shape   scuttlewords   deep sea venture words
words ringing in the diving bell and from beyond the man
with a gun shouting in the street
demanding papers and bigger than
julia-from-nebraska words   wreck survivor words
and suddenly the purpose returns

Someone Who

Not someone am I who knows each flower
in the garden by its true name.
& I am someone & you are someone & someone
knows where to bury the knife.
Why am I someone who knows what it means

to pray? I am someone who knows the lost-son way
she sighs, starves, cries
herself to sleep. Didn't anyone tell you? I know
what happened after
the cliff. I am someone who still knows how to give birth,

breath by breath by breath. When am I someone who
is willing to heal?
Who is (willing to create with what others have) discarded?
I am someone.
I am someone who is willing to greet the unpolished

Buddha inside you. Gentle, urgent, I am someone who
is willing to drink
from the mountain stream. Rubble-rust and unearthed iron
is what I am willing to start with.
I am/ someone/ who is/ willing to not/ go back/ to sleep.

THE OTHER SIDE OF OBLITERATION

when it's hard to
be kind to yourself
let me
be kind to you
if i am what you are
giving back to yourself
this small service
cannot be stopped even
as the forces of
denial are not so easily
shaken off everything that
aches can wake
you back up to this
Love
Everything

III

CLIMBING

At the base of the mountain,
we craned our necks upward
toward the peak.

We shed one comfort after another
to make the ascent.
Warm bed, sturdy walls,
market days, spare copies.
Citrus, apothecary—all gone.
A pilgrim lives
on what can be carried,
and often less
than that.

At the summit of the mountain,
we craned our necks upward
toward the stars.

We sang one song after another
to make the ascent.
Holy wind and water. Great Wheel
of Being. Granite guardians.
Friends of the mystery—all here.
A poet lives
on what can be worded
and often just
that.

WHEN YOU WERE BORN

When you were born,

>symphonies started playing, even though
>the conductors never showed.

>the broken vase jumped back onto the table
>to hold the daisies in place.

>all the teleprompters stopped working,
>and the fools went silent.

When you were born,

>the table was set for the feast,
>with Coyote as the guest of honor.

>wild salmon heard the First People dancing
>and leapt out of the water.

>the healers opened their palms to the heavens.

When you were born,

>the map scattered its perfectly plotted points
>into the sky, a new constellation, your name.

>something mysterious happened on the dune
>when no one was looking.

>the cracks in the arroyo connected to spell out
>the heart of every sacred scripture.

When you were born,

       salt shakers and teapots and iceboxes
       replenished themselves.

       the yellow lines on the road disappeared,
       the traffic lights all turned blue,
       and the speed limit signs read only "yes."

       those who had never before been able to say amen
       finally did.

When you were born, you knew why.

Nine Types of Silence

1.
We all share the same reason for being here.
The chairs are arranged in a circle.
The doctor seats herself in one of them.
The plastic creaks under her slight frame.
One girl swirls her coffee and takes a sip.
I watch her lipstick imprint itself on the lid.
If no one speaks, we won't have to acknowledge
what we know. If we stay silent, our stories
don't exist.

2.
He flicks his tail and takes two more steps
along the dusty ridge. The earth, a tinderbox below
his feet, cracking until he stops in his tracks.
Alarm brachycardia in us both. I swat the flies away
while he stands still, while his broken antler dangles
near his left eye. What do we see when we see
each other? Nothing rustles, not the birch leaf
mountain mahogany sunning itself along
one side of the trail, not a wisp of my hair. The sky
is mysteriously paused. Do his ears, *like wings
outstretched*, hear my heart-question?
He looks at me through the thick silence.
The creek below has long dried out,
and I turn back toward it, answerless.

3.
We can hold each other's gaze
from here to the green hillside.
We can choose to explain things
with our fingers or with stones.
We can hear the spider spinning
her web in the blackberry brambles
and wait for her to tell

her own story
of her own sky
and see ourselves in it.
While we say nothing, the grass
grows in our souls.

4.
I don't tell anyone about my collection. A poppy. A tulip. A
shoelace. A jar of nail polish. Emil's socks. The crest of the
mosaic. A discarded grocery list—don't forget the mayonnaise!
The stoplight at Central and Rengstorff. A glug of salsa picante
at the taqueria, where the men huddle around the small table
and forgo all chatter over lunch. Clara's ponytail holder. The
decadent roses, blooming just down the street. Blood, my blood.
The sacred words. The sacred wounds. A bookmark. A memory.

5.
There are scraps on the floor,
magazine clippings, postcards,
pages torn from books.
The hills turn to honey.
The streetlights come on. The moon
is tracking overhead.
The work is not finished.

6.
He was much older than I was, taller too. His shirt was
haphazardly tucked in, and the hems of his pants trailed the
ground a little as we walked, side-by-side, without looking at
each other. We turned left at the borage. We dipped under th
bougainvillea. We paused beneath the trellis. I had never met
him before, but here he was, telling me about the day his partner
was diagnosed with cancer, how his daughter once cut his hair
in his sleep, which direction he thought the clouds would roll in
from. His voice had mountains and valleys. His words were cliffs
and prairies. I lived in his landscapes without saying a word,
because that's what I was told to do. Is this a kind of love? The

teacher said that the listening space speaks through the speaker.
When it was my turn to share, I cried instead.

7.
We used to go for walks at night. We used to taunt
the darkness. Battered and reckless, we dragged
our bodies around, counting lights in distant windows,
giving ourselves ultimatums, asking for rain.
Deserted parking lots. Troubled thoughts. We read
accusations in the stars and found corroboration
in our scars. We hated our bodies so tenderly.
We despised our stories with such care.
A wayward hand at the piano bench.
A blood-stained mattress. A caged rooftop.
A knife at the throat. We never made a sound
when we slipped back inside, slid into bed,
let the ghosts hold court. Once, we dialed
the number of a friend who said
to reach out but hung up on the first ring.
What would they say if they knew:
we have been scythed by this brutal life,
we are choosing oblivion.

Gasp and grieve and disappear.

8.
A poem births itself out of a great silence.

> I recall "The Mower" and "Red Brocade"
> and make a simple vow inside my heart:
> I will be kind.

A poem flirts with the ripest silence.

> I cross the threshold to be with Wendell Berry
> and decide not to ask him a single question.

A poem creates a dazzling silence.

> *Ghost Of* lies open on my desk.
> Nox is its companion.
> My hands are bridging unspeakable losses.

A poem baffles.

> *I, too, have felt this furious light cascading through the epochs.*

9.
~~We are in a circle, afraid of our voices.~~
~~We are in the high meadow, begging the buck.~~
~~We are gardening and telling a story of growth.~~
~~We are gathering colors for the long winter.~~
~~We are bigger than our imaginings.~~
~~We are filling our pockets with the stories of strangers.~~
~~We are growling and howling inside.~~
~~We are smithers of whisper-words that caress the silence.~~
We are.

Simple Prayer

If there is not
a river
flowing in your
soul,
then pray
for water.
Your faith
will summon
the rain.
Give it time
to gather, collect
a current.
It will find a way
to lead you
to the sea.

Once the desire is truly there, the rest will resolve itself,
even in spite of you and your clumsy striving.

Every tear you cry along the way
baptizes the earth, declares all of it holy.

RIGHT HERE

People are trying to ask: where does joy still have
the courage to dance among the wild thistles and stand
wholeheartedly inside the sky? Darkness has become more
than just a word. It ripples in my throat. I lift my face, say
Right here.

A very polite poet paints the treetops with words
and puts a small bird on the uppermost branch.
I climb the stanzas, limb by limb,
in order to jump off and land
Right here.

Her shiver-song is an expression of a warmth-quest
as old as Jacob's ladder. Where is the heat that
heals more than what we dare to believe? I walk over
coals. The sacred fires are still burning, fierce, fiercer.
I place her hand on my chest, and my heart beats
Right here.

When the speaker proclaims their sound reasoning,
go ahead and listen. When it's your turn to respond,
and they demand to know on whose authority you stake
your claim, incline your head
Right here.

When the accuser points to the ground and marks
the spot of my assumed execution, I step lightly over
and place a circle of stones around my feet.
Right here.

Lazarus didn't beg for new life. He was simply in love
with his Lord. The banyan tree swayed silently
in the wind. Alyosha fell down and kissed
and kissed the earth. I offer my lips again,
Right here and here and here.

If they doubt that it's possible to be completely
annihilated *for love* and yet live, point
Right here.

Every birth is telling another story of how we met,
Right here.

Though I am not in Ligouri, I am taking a walk
among the wildflowers, and they are noisy. I cannot close
my ears to their shout-songs that God is
Right here.

Each time their young eyes search me,
combing the beach of this brutal world for a sign,
I look back at them from the sands of
Right here.

How hard did the angel squeeze until the scriptures came
pouring out?
Amen.

Who spoke first on the descent from Mount Tabor?
Amen.

Our tears are enough to wash away the soot
Right here.

When the beloved appears again
on the glowing green hillside,
the hollow trunks and rugged stones will
remember how to call themselves
altars, proclaiming at every moment that
all we need is
Right here.

THE POET REVISITS HERSELF IN SPRING

The northern mockingbirds have returned
again and made a nest in the bush
at the edge of the driveway. The poet watches
the children cluster around and coo at the babies, tie
bits of string around the branches in celebration
and make a bed of leaves and poppy petals below,
should one of the fledglings meet gravity
before their earth-wings are ready.
A troupe of males triangulate their watch:
rooftop, lamppost, telephone wire. Their
calls have become unmistakable.
The poet is always here, taking notes, which
is to say is always here, taking in — the single lupine
and the dead lamb's ear, the green platter
succulents from Lily's fenceless garden and all
the seeds that have not yet found a way
to be licked alive by the sun. Grey-breasted
birds stay a while and go, and whatever is born
eventually finds its own legs and walks a
way. Growing things takes courage, kairos.
Rice husks dissolve in the soil like yesterdays,
and the poet thinks there are only two kinds of time:
the back-then of belief and the fresh-now of faith.
The planets will not wash their hands
of what is trying to emerge here along all these
fault lines, here among these faulty minds.
The poet is constellating her tender-tongued
self into every season.

The Crossing

these heights are not
for the you that is reading
there is some
other you
    alter christus
        that you will have become
        without having left
        the place where you stand

to cross the threshold
first undread the truth
embodied composite
behold what you have
fearfully and wonderfully made
with your hands that
you must train
    not to tremble
        not to grasp at
            elaborate rituals built on
                rows of beeswax votives
                singing crystal bowls
                leather phylacteries
                fired ceramic tasbih
                burnt offerings
                medieval cornerstones
                consecrated in some other
                annus domini

now is your time to begin with nothing

but an open heart
in the patient vessel you are navigating
should you take to furious paddling
        with your destination-eager right hand

cut it off and cast it from you
      cosmic tides
      are here as guides
      slow going in the
      direction of destiny
      under orion's arrow
      the pull of the brightest star

and a willing mind
    disposed to discarding all daydreams
    mental meanderings
    eager to pursue
only upright thoughts

something attentive in you had called you this far
you don't know what to call it yet
but you will

Rossmoor Bar

Let me remind you who you are, says the river
at dawn.

She lets off steam, and I bless the fog my body releases.
She exhales, and I marvel at my breath shapeshifting
in the air. She flows, and I go deeper into the universal rhythm of
my footfall. She borrows from the eye of the blue heron, the call
of the osprey, the sharp and silky scales of the trout, and so do I.
All aswirl in the Great Becoming.

We watch together as a royal cascade of color
floods the treetops and kisses the bellies of birds,
turning their feathers to gold as they fly.
We are ready when the Sun Being once more
touches down on the dew-damp earth, a promise
and a peace offering that she understands better
than I.

What should I call this waiting? For a moment,
River and Light and I speak the same language,
and the only word we need is *thanksgiving*.

TRIDUUM

i. cenacle

my daughter and i stand at the skillet,
crackling oil at its smoking point.
we are sturdy. we have plenty.
she lifts the edge of the charred bread with
kitchen tongs to marvel at the color it takes.
we wait to flip it until just before it burns. it's
the closest we get to eating fire.

this bread is leavened, yes.
what does she know of eating affliction, of
stunted loaves, all sun-stained and unable
to rise. and me? that taste is fading now.

these feet are clean, yes.
what does she know of the everlasting sand, the slow-
going of the desert and the fear-faith that
causes some to flee. and me? that route is losing its coordinates.

i retain the questions. is it wrong to skirt these inheritances?
is life bittersweet or sweetbitter? who is the modern
miller? what is mine to do?

this table is set, yes. we give thanks.

ii. lama sabachthani

i am   a friend of this
Mystery.

to be this way in one's body: splayed
out, pierced through, bloodied at the hands of Man.
amazed at the monstrous warmth
of my own riverblood, wine-dark
for some

time lost
beneath its unstoppable flow
uncertain of ever emerging from its throes

i rendered my Spirit.

the body as a cross-
roads of what shouldn't have to be
and what is.

iii. the vigil approaches

who can say to the shrieking one: i am
not rattled by your pain. i am
not afraid of the lacerations. i am
not too weary to listen listen listen listen wait listen
we can keep the nightwatch at the hillside
we can bear the wilderness
we can limp toget-
her, away from here

did anyone remain at the place
of the skull? at the tomb?
even the mother went home to
small comforts, privately
reckon   with the truth
of what she saw, sees without knowing what would come
of it. fear and doubt are not
yet cast into the sea. she freshens the linens.

even so someone must fill the amphora. come,
the oil is waiting to be of use, all of creation
is waiting, wanting to heal. there is great need of
anointing.
there is no other future.

AT THE CREEK

1.
each shadow a small
promise of what can still be
revealed: way-making light.

2.
earth altars, nosegays:
honeysuckle, white sage, pine.
i need my body.

3.
we follow the deer tracks
to the black cottonwood tree
and wait in silence.

4.
my breath catches at
each feather. what has happened
to my winter wings?

5.
i offer myself
a bouquet of rosemary,
wind, and wild prayers.

The Sand Speaks

Didn't we empty the Great Glassblower's bowl
of wine and dance in it until it shattered?

Why scramble to pick up the pieces? It is not suitable
to handle broken glass with bare hands. Did you see

the doves turn into stars? Are you suddenly ashamed
of what we've done? The former vessel is not meant

to be reconstituted. Chosenness cannot be destroyed.
How many times must I bow down to be completely

beheaded? Can you hear me telling a story about death,
which is also resurrection? The stones roll through

open windows. There's no such thing
as loss. The beet greens wilt in the sizzling butter,

and my body becomes as impermanent as it is.
When did I lose my patience for merely sayable things?

My beloved needed something to hold onto so I tied
the whole world together with a red string. Why should

I care if one chooses to snip themselves free? The gift
has been given. How much longer will this annihilation last?

Which of the figs will ripen? Possible is still too small
for me. I trace the questions in the sand and they withstand the

tides. Did Lazarus become John? The cocoon dissolves
completely. The cloud gives way to rain. What does my

righteous gospel do to the soul who hears? I am a seed,
scattered on the wise wind, the Great Glassblower's

breath, about to touch down in the field
of lover-lilacs and stay. When I take root and feed

on the sky, will that prove my point?
Have I already reached beyond the point of prooflessness?

Epiphany

I took my body down to the river
I took my body behind the bushes

slipped off my shoes and all my black clothes this is not
a funeral I put on a red dress, the blushing that my skin has

not known how to allow the blood that I have not learned to trust
I wore it outside my body to try and understand

what is inside my body I give it all to the last rays of sun
at the darkest time of year at the feast of enlightenment

who will offer me gold frankincense myrrh
if not my own clumsy hands

I took my body to the river's edge,
let it be led to the whirlpool

to the place where current came back to itself
turned in on itself and still somehow found its way

into the flow once again
A wise one told me to let the warmth

move all the way through my body
and more give it to the earth all the way down so I tried

my feet resting on the riverbed
the place that is both receiving and releasing

at every moment, holds everything keeps nothing
and how can I not turn this into a metaphor how can I

stand the pain of being this here and gone
this one sweetwater drop on its way to the unknowable sea

I pulled my body back from the river
with a red stone in my hand for the red love she lets me
hold and wept again for the heat I fear I'll never find
without the voice that covers me

I am lost at the wild river
in this too-small moment
in this monstrously miraculous moment
in this shedding and scorching silkworm moment

I am found at the wild river
in this amaresynthesis moment
in this skipping stones and laying on of hands moment
in this unspeakable obliteration of what time

has and has not healed, I am

Found Miracles

for Thich Nhat Hanh

i.
Tolstoy is a saint. How?
A person who looks at the table
and can see the universe is
a person who can see the way.

ii.
The body bloats and turns violet,
is eaten by worms.
Only white bones remain,
slowly turn to dust.

iii.
When I was 19 years old,
we had no soap. There was only ashes,
rice husks, coconut husks,
and nothing else. We are
incapable of realizing the miracle
of life while standing at the sink.

iv.
I was worried whether
he could endure the four walls
of the prison. "Do you remember
the tangerine we shared
when we were together?" To think
in terms of either pessimism
or optimism simplifies the truth.

v.
This is your own time.
The spot where you sit is your spot.
Why put so much stress on a simple thing?
But that is precisely the point.

vi.
The raft is used to cross the river.
It isn't meant to be carried
around your shoulders. Of all
the people who have passed
by your yard, how many
have really seen the almond tree?

vii.
Be like a medieval knight
walking weaponless
in a forest of swords.
What counts
is your own heart.

ALL THESE HOLY NAMES

Amaranth seeds, a gift on a Monday afternoon.
The swallow and the thrush.
Q: What is sunlight made of? A: Photons.
All the reds in every Matisse painting, recklessly alive.
A ring around just one finger, the middle one.
Sap, singing marrow.
Blood, hot thick on a mission.
Cataracts in rivers, in eyes. Obstacles are natural, essential.
The kumquat sapling I've yet to acquire.
Riding without training wheels.
Pranayama.
The kiss of the finger pad on the rose-scented beads.
Sheared wool atop the compost heap.
G-chord, no capo. Open tuning too.
Switching off the light and saying goodnight.
I put my hand in the urn. I used a plastic shell
      to scoop out her ashes and
      pour them into the opening in the ground.
      At the pulpit, I spoke about intimacy
      with death, and now I touched it,
      at least, the remnants of it.
      I was the only one.
      The breeze caught up with us,
      with the geraniums and their flashes
      of fuschia and red. Like in the garden bed
      she once tended, like in the hanging pots
      that once dotted the patio. All of this, all of her,
      Gone. Beyond. Away. This breeze is her breath now.
      Does anyone else know it?
Participation.

In the Time Before and Again Now

Before we lived in the world of things we lived in each
other. I don't just mean me and you but me and all

any every other you. The you of the buzzing chaparral
where the bees find a feast every spring. The you

of the sacred hoop of history. The you of hedge apples
falling with a thud upon the still frosted earth. The you that

is most alive in the dance of the light at dusk. The you that
tendrils out into the bright morning on the other

side of whatever the moon had to say. The canyon you,
the canopy you, the rush of frigid rain and feather-breasted

you. But we have come into the world of things
just as surely as we have been given names.

This is what the supposedly clever ones call growing
up. The dishes are stacked neatly in the cupboard and the

papers have been filed away. Someone has already drawn
the curtains closed. Yet sometimes the wind knocks on the

door and stirs me from my sleep. I go to open what another has
shut and find myself face to face with apple blossoms

laughing in the night. I think. I think,
Ah, here we are again, weaving.

DISCERNMENT

winnow
as indeed we must
but know:
both the wheat
and the chaff
are useful

no thing without purpose are we
given
we need fuel for the
fire
to bake the
bread
we are called to

                                  break

in remembrance of
that
Love

A Passion

i.
the be held and to behold / are an initiation / this is how it
begins / if we are / at a beginning / something must also be /
ending / this is the end of eyes / this is the start / of sight //

ii.
i wept alone in the garden / beside the guava tree / the olives
of gethsemane / were far from me now / but the dark night was
the same / the others caviled / just beyond the hedge / trading
pleasantries and judgments / i could see their bodies / moving
but they were deep / in sleep / i prayed i prayed i / prayed / i
prayed into the black bowl of stars overhead / what is it to be on
this earth? //

iii.
i could have walked / the whole journey on my knees / spilling
blood no longer alarms me / haven't i been conditioned / to fall
down / before the mighty? haven't i been taught to call myself
weak? / the earth-bound enthusiasm of the crowds has died /
down and the streets are empty now / and i go lovingly into such
doom / as only i can / must shoulder //

iv.
in the bed in outer sunset / no one saw / his eyes were closed
/ my eyes were closed / neither of us knew the color / of the
monstrosity until later / i was laid / out torn / through /
abandoned / on the hill / i rushed into a tomb of my own
making / for years my body / made appearances / on the other
side / but always went back to the grave / no one saw / not even
me // i'm getting another chance / now to make the ascent /
to embrace the execution / this time out of love / out of free
surrender / to place a placard above my battered body that reads
/ *this suffering is not — who i am — but who — i am — is someone who
accepts — this suffering* //

v.
that one tried to wash his hands of me / that one kept pouring
fresh water in the basin / that one tried to mount the case against
me / that one tried to trap me with floral-scented questions and
flaunted the protocols / my preaching my teaching my message
my love / unreceivable / that one wonders whether to believe me
/ that one is still trying to rile the crowd / assemble the rabble /
break my bastion-body / that one is telling everyone to go home
/ that one can't be convinced to walk away / those ones will one
day / have to reckon with / their misplaced desires / for now
they have done their job / well because i no longer / want to go
to sleep / and now those ones watch me fall / to my knees / and
remind me that my legs aren't / broken / i decline the terms of
the game / and play until / i decide / it is finished //

vi.
you've never seen / love like this before / you've never seen power
/ refuse to dominate / you've never had to look into the well /
the chalice / the jug / the fountain / and find such latent evil /
where living water / should be / you've never dared believe that
nothing / was the answer / that emptiness was the solution / that
getting it right could hurt / you've never been asked to raise your
eyes beyond the dust / but here / i am / on the hill / and you
can't look away / listen to me refuse / those small consolations /
agonize / pray a prayer you / can hardly imagine / *forgive them* //
only the sleep-walking malice missionaries / and soul-shattered
beloveds / remain which one / are you //

vii.
for the stories / he was willing to tell / about the least / among us
the woman / at the well / the overlooked outcast / for the hands
/ he laid on this blistered breasts / and blood-forsaken feet / and
corrupt but contrite souls / for the wounds he was willing to kiss
/ for the love made visible in his eyes / they have come to kill
him / he wept / and then said yes // for the stories / i am willing
to tell / about the great chain of being / and the seeds that
belong to rocks / for the hearts i have gathered / at the gate of

enchantment / for the hate i refuse / to ingest for the battle i fight / without a single weapon / for the dreams / in which we say yes / and mean it / they have come / to kill me / so i weep too / and then say yes //

viii.
if someone must be blamed / blame me / if someone must be mocked / mock me / if someone must be eliminated / eliminate me / this is how / i prayed my prayer / is being answered / i choose / this death / for what it is / the end of a lie / the birth of my first / freedom //

ACKNOWLEDGMENTS

Even though my children are still too young to understand that they helped me become a writer and an artist, they are the first people I want to thank for their contributions to this book. Kamden, you rescued me from the world of abstractions. There is almost no better feeling than sitting side-by-side in bed, each writing in our notebooks. Thank you for loving words and me. Ayelet, you gave me a new body and brave heart. Your freedom is one of my greatest teachers. When you were born, you knew why. Thank you also to Tony, who helps me remember, whenever I forget, that I was born to live in the fire.

There are places that held me through the creation of this collection, places without which I wouldn't be a human being, much less a writer. Thank you, McClellan Ranch, Blackberry Farm, Rancho San Antonio open space preserve, the American River Parkway, and Waldorf schools, for holding me when I was in freefall. Your bucks and rocks and community gardens brimming with zinnia and pattypan squash and whole-making souls are the reason I'm still here.

Finally, thank you to Ruth Thompson, for your eye for images and for trusting me to learn trust my readers, and Don Mitchell, for being an atheist who's fond of masses and making magic on the pages of my book. You both took a chance on a first-time, self-taught poet, and I am so grateful.

Most of Part I was published in chapbook form as *Wild Canvas* (Finishing Line Press, 2024).

"throwing seeds at rocks" was published by *Wild Roof Journal*

"Summer Winds Nursery" was published in *Beyond Queer Words*

"In the Liminal Mo(u)rning" was published by *Beyond Words Literary Magazine*

"Nine Types of Silence" was published in *Sad Girl Diaries*

"A Passion" was published in *Pensive: A Global Journal of Spirituality and the Arts*

"At the Creek" and "The Poet Revisits Herself in Spring" were published in *Willows Wept*

"Bloodlines" was published in *The Central Dissent: A Journal of Gender and Sexuality (New Plains Review)*

"Unannounced Guest" was published in *Viewless Wings*

About the Author

Alison Davis is an award-winning educator, scholar, artist, and activist based in Northern California. Alison's work has been featured in a wide range of literary and scholarly publications, including *The Sun, Rattle, Pensive: A Global Journal of Spirituality and the Arts, Braided Way, SAUTI: Stanford Journal of African Studies, Research Bulletin*, and *School Renewal*, as well as the chapbook *Wild Canvas* (Finishing Line Press, 2024).

Although she holds multiple advanced degrees from Very Prestigious Universities, she sees her willingness to be like Rumi and gamble everything for love as her greatest credential. *A Rare But Possible Condition* is her debut collection.